A CourseGuide for

Christ Alone

Stephen Wellum

**ZONDERVAN
ACADEMIC**

ZONDERVAN ACADEMIC

A CourseGuide for Christ Alone

Copyright © 2020 by Zondervan

Requests for information should be addressed to:
Zondervan, *3900 Sparks Dr. SE, Grand Rapids, Michigan 49546*

ISBN 978-0-310-11018-7 (softcover)

Printed in the United States of America

CONTENTS

Introduction

Welcome to *A CourseGuide for Christ Alone*. These guides were created for formal and informal students alike who want to engage deeper in biblical, theological, or ministry studies. We hope this guide will provide an opportunity for you to grow not only in your understanding, but also in your faith.

How to Use This Guide

This guide is meant to be used in conjunction with the book *Christ Alone — The Uniqueness of Jesus as Savior* and its corresponding videos, *Christ Alone Video Lectures*. After you have read each chapter in the book and watched the accompanying video lesson, the materials in this guide will help you review and assess what you have learned. Application-oriented questions are included as well.

Each CourseGuide has been individually designed to best equip you in your studies, but in general, you can expect the following components. Most CourseGuides begin every chapter with a "You Should Know" section, which highlights key terminology, people, and facts to remember. This section serves as a helpful summary for directing your studies. Reflection questions, typically two to three per chapter, prompt you to summarize key points you've learned. Discussion questions invite you to an even deeper level of engagement. Finally, most chapters will end with a short quiz to test your retention. You can find the answer key to each quiz at the bottom of the page following it.

For Further Study

CourseGuides accompany books and videos from some of the world's top biblical and theological scholars. They may be used independently, or in small groups or classrooms, offering quality instruction to equip students for academic and ministry pursuits. If you would like to engage in further study with Zondervan's CourseGuides, the full lineup may be viewed online. After completing your studies with *A CourseGuide for Christ Alone*, we recommend moving on to *A Course-Guide for God's Glory Alone* and *A CourseGuide for God's Word Alone*.

Introduction to
Christ Alone

You Should Know

- "*Solus Christus* stands at the center of the other four *solas*, connecting them into a coherent theological system by which the Reformers declared the glory of God."

- We come to know the person and work of Christ by God's self-disclosure through Scripture.

- According to Michael Reeves, "to be truly Trinitarian we must be constantly Christ-centered."

- *Christ alone* must connect all the doctrines of Christian theology because Christ alone is the cornerstone of all the purposes and plans of God.

- The English translations of the five Reformation *solas*: Scripture alone, God's glory alone, grace alone, faith alone, Christ alone

- The two teachings that should guide our insights into the Reformers' understanding of *Christ alone*: the exclusive identity of Christ and the sufficient work of Christ

Essay Questions

Short

1. Why did the Reformers place *Christ alone* at the center of their doctrine of Scripture?

2. Why is Christ alone the key to the coherence of Christian teaching?

3. Why is it important today to learn from the Reformers' emphasis on Christ alone?

Long

1. How does *Christ alone* relate to the doctrines of the Trinity, humanity, salvation, and atonement? Can you think of any other doctrines that are best understood in the context of *Christ alone*?

Quiz

1. (T/F) Reformation theology is often summarized by the five *solas*.

2. (T/F) John Calvin wrote that "Christology is the true hub round which the wheel of theology revolves."

3. (T/F) The incarnation is indispensable to the atonement.

4. (T/F) Exploring the doctrine of *Christ alone* is a lifelong pursuit.

5. _____ is at the center of the Reformation *solas* and at the heart of Christian theology.

    a) Grace alone
    b) Faith alone
    c) Scripture alone
    d) Christ alone

6. The Reformers confessed that _____ is the focus of all God's work in the world.

    a) The Holy Spirit
    b) Christ
    c) Scripture
    d) The Church

7. Reformed theologian _____ wrote that the doctrine of Christ is "the central point of the whole system of dogmatics."

    a) Herman Bavinck
    b) Alister McGrath
    c) Stephen Wellum
    d) B. B. Warfield

8. The church confesses the triunity of God because Scripture reveals the divine Son's _____. (p. 23)

    a) Liberation
    b) Exaltation
    c) Incarnation
    d) Resurrection

9. *Solus Christus* is Latin for _____.

    a) The soul of Christ
    b) Christ alone
    c) Christ the Son
    d) The salvation of Christ

10. What Christ has done is directly related to _____.

    a) What he wants
    b) Who he has called
    c) Who he is
    d) Where he ministered

CHAPTER 1

The Biblical Identity of Jesus Christ

You Should Know

- The God of Scripture is the triune Creator-Covenant Lord.

- The most *new* about the new covenant is the promise of complete forgiveness of sin.

- The primary message of the covenants is that unless God himself acts to accomplish his promises, we have no salvation.

- The four major pieces to the puzzle of Christ's identity and his accomplishments: who God is; what he requires of humans; why sin creates a problem between God and humans; how God himself provides the solution to the problem between God and humans

- Fatalism: God is under an external necessity to act as he does in salvation

- Two major Old Testament eschatological expectations that unite in Christ: Christ is the sovereign Lord who comes to save his people and Christ is David's greater Son

Essay Questions

Short

1. In regard to the necessity of Christ for salvation, explain the difference between hypothetical necessity and consequent absolute necessity. Which view of necessity do you favor at this point, and why?

2. How did the human race become sinful? Does Adam bear all of the blame for individual sins today?

3. Why is Jesus's identity as the Messiah important for salvation? Why must the Messiah be both God and man?

Long

1. In what ways does the Old Testament predict and foreshadow Jesus's life, ministry, death, and resurrection?

Quiz

1. (T/F) Our understanding of who Jesus is and what he does must be developed primarily from the Gospels.

2. (T/F) God is part of the world and develops along with it.

3. (T/F) The Lord created and covenanted with Adam for the purpose of bearing God's image in human dominion over creation.

4. (T/F) In the Old Testament, all of the covenant mediators fail and do not fulfill God's promises.

5. (T/F) The primary message of the covenants is that unless God cooperates with human beings, we have no salvation.

6. At the heart of *solus Christus* is the confession that the salvation of humanity depends upon the _____ and _____ of Christ.

    a) Origin / Destiny
    b) Teachings / Miracles
    c) Person / Work
    d) Sermons / Parables

7. _____ wrote: "I have with sorrow become more afraid of the word 'Jesus' than almost any other word in the modern world."

    a) D. A. Carson
    b) J. I. Packer
    c) David Wells
    d) Francis Schaeffer

8. Jesus reconciled _____ and grace in his cross.

    a) Divine justice
    b) Divine love
    c) Faith
    d) Hope

9. In _____, Adam disobeys God and God expels Adam and his wife from the garden.

    a) Exodus 3
    b) Psalm 3
    c) Genesis 12
    d) Genesis 3

10. In Christ, all of the biblical covenants reach their _____.

    a) Terminus
    b) Beginning
    c) Midpoint
    d) Capacity

CHAPTER 2

The Self-Witness of Christ: God the Son Incarnate

You Should Know

- God alone is worthy of worship because of his metaphysical-moral perfections.

- By referring to himself as "I am" Jesus communicated that he connected his personal identity with Yahweh.

- The NT presents Jesus as a model of faith in his relationship as a man with God.

- Word: an Old Testament term closely associated with God who is active in creation, revelation, and redemption

- The five most significant aspects of Jesus's earthly life that reveal his self-identity: his baptism, the kingdom he inaugurated, his life and ministry, his death and resurrection, and the worship he received

- Three things Jesus, as the Son of God, knew he would accomplish through his death: Bring divine judgment upon the world, depose Satan as "the ruler of this world," and install himself as king over all creation for the sake of all people

Essay Questions

Short

1. What do Jesus's teachings and miracles reveal about his unique identity? What did he mean when he said he came to fulfill the law?

2. How do Jesus's death and resurrection demonstrate his identity as God the Son?

3. What does Jesus communicate about his identity as the Son of God in John 5:19–23? What does the title "Son of Man" tell us about Jesus's identity?

Long

1. What is at stake in the question of Jesus's identity? What difference does it make that he is God and not merely human?

Quiz

1. (T/F) Jesus knew that he was both God and man.

2. (T/F) Instead of self-identity, we should think in terms of Jesus's self-consciousness.

[The opposite is true.]

3. (T/F) Jesus's death was planned before the foundation of the world.

4. (T/F) Jesus explicitly says in the Gospels that he is God the Son incarnate.

5. (T/F) The words of Christ give us hermeneutical instruction from our covenantal head on how to understand the contours of his identity and work.

6. The Gospel of John declares that the Word shares the intrinsic nature of God and eternally exists in _____ with God.

   a) Personal intercommunion
   b) Timeless stasis
   c) Frequent contact
   d) Changing phases

7. The New Testament presents the works of Jesus as _____ greater than everything that has preceded him.

   a) Somewhat
   b) Fewer but

c) Qualitatively

d) Reluctantly

8. _____ and _____ are the sole prerogatives of God.

a) Faith / Love

b) Resurrection / Judgment

c) Power / Glory

d) Time / Space

9. In Daniel 7, the _____ takes on the significance of a superhuman figure who functions alongside the Ancient of Days.

a) Son of Man

b) Son of God

c) Son of Adam

d) Son of Eve

10. Jesus makes all of the following "I am" statements except:

a) The Bread of Life

b) The True Vine

c) The Gate

d) The Son of David

CHAPTER 3

The Apostolic Witness to Christ: God the Son Incarnate

You Should Know

- Jesus's works and words in the context of kingdom promises tell us that Jesus is the divine Son, the Creator-Covenant Lord.

- The transition from Romans 1:3 to 1:4 is not a transition from a human messiah to a divine Son of God (adoptionism) but from the Son as Messiah to the Son as both Messiah *and* powerful, reigning Lord.

- Paul emphasizes that Jesus did not take advantage of or exploit the equality with God that he already possessed.

- The four key texts covered in this section that provide the main apostolic witness to Christ's unique identity: Romans 1:3–4, Philippians 2:5–11, Colossians 1:15–20, and Hebrews 1:1–3

- The chronological sequence of the Son's relation to creation in Colossians 1:16: the past—the Son is the agent of creation; the present: the world owes its allegiance to the Son; the future — the Son's sovereignty will become universal

- Five crucial identity statements about the Son that the author of Hebrews communicates in Hebrews 1:2–3: the Son is the heir of all things; the Son is the agent of creation; the Son is God the Son and fully God; the Son is the Lord of providence; and the Son is the all-sufficient Redeemer

Essay Questions

Short

1. Describe the difference between "ontological" and "functional" Christology. Why is this distinction not helpful?

2. What basic, unified pattern does the apostolic witness to Jesus's sonship follow?

3. How should we understand Paul's statement that Christ is "the first-born of all creation"? How does this relate to the Arian controversy?

Long

1. Choose one point from each of the four key texts in this section (Rom. 1:3–4; Phil. 2:5–11; Col. 1:15–20; Heb. 1:1–3) and explain what it communicates about Jesus's identity.

Quiz

1. (T/F) Jesus's own words and works form the theological foundation for the apostles' witness to his exclusive identity.

2. (T/F) "Functional" Christology is identified with classical Christology as represented by the Chalcedonian definition.

3. (T/F) James Dunn argues that Jesus was not the eternal Son but became the Son at his resurrection.

4. (T/F) God the Son incarnate is the antitype of the sons of the Old Testament.

5. (T/F) Saying that Christ has always existed in the "form of God" (Phil. 2:6) is another way of saying that Jesus is one of God's special creations.

6. (T/F) Hebrews 1:1–2 indicates that Old Testament revelation is inferior to the revelation brought by the Son, Jesus Christ.

7. There is debate over whether Philippians 2:5–11 is a _____ or original to Paul.

    a) Forgery

    b) Later addition

    c) Copyist mistake

    d) Pre-Pauline hymn

8. The Father bestows on Christ the name above all names, which is his own name, _____.

    a) God

    b) Yahweh

    c) Deity

    d) Father

9. The Son stands at the beginning as the _____ of creation and at the end as the _____ of creation.

    a) Agent / Goal

    b) Spirit / Father

    c) Receiver / Giver

    d) Watcher / Workman

10. The entire book of Hebrews is centered in _____.

    a) Metaphor

    b) Christology

    c) Pneumatology

    d) Creation

CHAPTER 4

From Incarnation to Atonement: An Exclusive Identity for an All-Sufficient Work

You Should Know

- According to J. I. Packer, the "supreme mystery with which the gospel confronts us" is why God became man.

- Through death, Jesus destroys death.

- The grave was unable to hold Christ because he overcame death in a great battle after his crucifixion; he was assisted by the angels who ministered to him; he ascended into heaven because he had his Father's permission; his death paid for sin in full, leaving no cause for death; he put aside everything related to his previous, earthly life

- "Because he himself suffered when he was tempted, he is able to help those who are being tempted" (Hebrews 2:18).

- Three things at the center of God's eternal plan to redeem humanity: restoring humanity to our image-bearing role; bringing us into a new and better covenant relationship with our Creator-Covenant Lord; and providing atonement that results in the forgiveness of sins

- The four-part rationale the author of Hebrews develops in Hebrews 2:5–18 for the necessity and inseparability of Christ's incarnation and atonement: God the Son becomes man to fulfill

God's original intention for humanity; God the Son became a man to bring many sons to glory; God the Son became a man to destroy the power of death and the Devil; God the Son became a man to become a merciful and faithful high priest

Essay Questions

Short

1. In your own words, summarize the six points of the biblical rationale for the necessity of Christ's incarnation and atonement.

2. Why is the forgiveness of sins the focal point of God's redemptive plan?

3. How did God the Son become a merciful and faithful high priest for us (see Hebrews 2:17–18)? Why was it necessary for the Son to become flesh in order to be our perfect high priest?

Long

1. According to the storyline of Scripture, what is our greatest problem as fallen creatures? What state or condition does God intend to restore us to? What role does Jesus's incarnation play in this restoration?

Quiz

1. (T/F) Christ's incarnation was not an end in itself, but a means of fulfilling his mission.

2. (T/F) Death is only our enemy because we are sinners before God.

3. (T/F) The Son did not have to become like us in every way to redeem us in every way.

4. (T/F) Jesus knows our temptations and struggles through omniscience, but not by experience.

5. (T/F) Adam's human role could only be restored by an obedient Son acting as our representative.

6. _____ famously asked, "Why did God become man?"

   a) Augustine
   b) Anselm of Canterbury
   c) Martin Luther
   d) Billy Graham

7. The Son has fulfilled all of God's promises, especially those associated with the _____ covenant.

   a) Davidic
   b) Adamic
   c) Abrahamic
   d) Noahic

8. Psalm 8 celebrates the majesty of God as the Creator and the _____ humans have in creation.

   a) Challenging issues
   b) Joyful experiences
   c) Many responsibilities
   d) Exalted position

9. _____ is the only one who has genuinely lived the kind of life that humans were intended to live under God.

   a) Adam
   b) Moses
   c) Jesus
   d) Paul

10. Hebrews 2:10 says that God made Jesus "perfect through what he suffered." The term "perfect" here is best understood _____.

   a) Vocationally
   b) Relationally
   c) Globally
   d) Concretely

ANSWER KEY

1. T, 2. T, 3. F, 4. F, 5. T, 6. B, 7. A, 8. D, 9. C, 10. A

CHAPTER 5

The Threefold Office of Christ Alone: Our Prophet, Priest, King

You Should Know

- A prophet, according to Scripture, is a "man of God" who speaks God's word to the people.

- The meaning of *logos* is found in the Old Testament, where "word of God" is associated with creation, revelation, redemption, and God himself.

- The old covenant priests offered the blood of animals on behalf of human sinners so that the Lord could dwell with Israel without destroying it.

- Christ's resurrection is evidence that his work to save his people from their sins has been achieved.

- Three reasons why it helps to consider the sufficiency of Christ's work in terms of his threefold office of prophet, priest, and king: The threefold office of Christ comes from the covenantal-typological development of the biblical storyline to demonstrate how Christ functions as our covenantal mediator and why his work is superior; the threefold office of Christ shows us the comprehensive nature of both sin's corruption and Christ's salvation; the threefold office of Christ summarizes and integrates the biblical data on all that Christ has done to fulfill God's plans and purposes.

- The unfolding of the prophetic ministry of Christ includes: the first years he spent with his disciples; the writings of the apostles of Christ; and the contemporary work of the Spirit of Christ who illuminates the church for reading the Scriptures

- Three reasons why priestly mediation is necessary for our salvation: we have sinned against the holy and just Creator-Covenant Lord; God's forgiveness of our sins requires the death of a representative substitute who bears our sins; the Lord has promised to provide a representative substitute for us

Essay Questions

Short

1. What is the basic function of a prophet? How does Christ fulfill the function of a prophet and provide the prophetic word we need for our salvation?

2. What is the basic function of a priest in Scripture? Explain three ways that Christ is greater than priests in the Old Testament. How is Christ's new priesthood superior to the entire Levitical system?

3. What is the basic function of a king in Scripture? Why is the lordship of a king necessary for our salvation? How does Christ's ascension relate to his role as king?

Long

1. Why is it helpful to consider the sufficiency of Christ's work in terms of his threefold office of prophet, priest, and king? Which of Christ's three offices (prophet, priest, king) is most neglected in the church today? How should we address the deficiency?

Quiz

1. (T/F) The sin of the first Adam has affected every aspect of humanity.

2. (T/F) Isaiah promised that one day the Lord would raise up another prophet like him.

3. (T/F) Christ's prophetic work continues from the throne of heaven through the apostles and Scriptures.

4. (T/F) The Old Testament prophets did not explicitly speak of the third person of the Trinity.

5. The sufficiency of Christ as our prophet, priest, and king is a biblical truth that was developed by _____ and the heirs of the Reformation.

    a) J. I. Packer

    b) Origen

    c) John Calvin

    d) D. L. Moody

6. From a Christian worldview, _____ is possible because it is grounded in the triune God.

    a) Scripture

    b) Truth

    c) The Church

    d) History

7. The author of Hebrews describes priests as _____ between a sinful people and their holy God.

    a) Mediators

    b) Obstacles

    c) Communicators

    d) Helpers

8. God designed the Old Testament sacrificial system to be both _____ and _____.

    a) Theological / Theoretical

    b) Historical / Contemporary

    c) Merciful / Just

    d) Typological / Temporary

9. _____ famously wrote that "There is not a square inch in the whole domain of our human existence over which Christ, who is Sovereign over all, does not cry: 'Mine!'"

   a) John Calvin
   b) D. L. Moody
   c) John Stott
   d) Abraham Kuyper

10. _____ is the culmination of Christ's earthly work by which he inaugurated the new covenant age.

   a) Pentecost
   b) Prophecy
   c) The New Testament
   d) The Great Commission

CHAPTER 6

The Cross-Work of Christ in Historical Perspective

You Should Know

- One significant reason that the early church did not convene a council to settle the doctrine of the atonement is that the basic understanding of the cross was taken for granted.

- The Reformers and their heirs viewed sin primarily as a violation of God's holy and righteous character.

- "The moral law does not function 'outside' of God; rather God *is* the law, and as such, he is the universal, objective standard of justice."

- Three reasons Anselm's *Why God Became Man* was one of the most significant theological treatments of the atonement in the medieval era: it was largely responsible for moving the church from the ransom theory to the satisfaction view of the cross; it was a major attempt to give a rational and theological account of the atonement by reflecting on the necessity of the cross; it developed earlier views and brought more precision to the proper object of the cross, God himself

- Aseity: God's independence and complete personal self-sufficiency

- Divine voluntarism: God's choices depend only on what he wills, and not on his nature

Essay Questions

Short

1. Why is it misleading to say that the church has no unity in its understanding of the cross?

2. How does John Calvin's view of the atonement contrast with and improve upon Anselm's view of the atonement?

3. In the penal substitution view of the atonement, what is the theological significance of the terms "penal" and "substitution"?

Long

1. Briefly summarize and explain the theories of atonement described in this section. What positive aspects do you see in the theories discussed in this section?

Quiz

1. (T/F) The boundaries and content of atonement theology became especially clear during the Reformation and post-Reformation eras.

2. (T/F) Athanasius understood the necessity of the cross in terms of Christ bearing our curse in order to defeat the power of sin and death.

3. (T/F) Penal substitution emphasizes that Christ died primarily in order to provide a moral example to God's people.

4. (T/F) Anselm pointed out that part of our human condition is that we have nothing to give God in recompense for sin.

5. (T/F) The Reformers rejected the Trinitarian and christological thought of the patristic and medieval eras.

6. (T/F) The governmental theory argues that Christ's death is absolutely necessary, not hypothetically necessary.

7. _____ wrote: "It is not enough to maintain that Christ's Priesthood is a real and veritable office; it must be regarded and set forth as pre-eminently *the* office—the foundation office—which Christ as Redeemer executes."

   a) Hugh Martin
   b) John Calvin
   c) Martin Luther
   d) Donald Macleod

8. Scripture declares the priority of God's _____ as the reason he takes the initiative to save us.

   a) Justice and righteousness
   b) Power and authority
   c) Love and grace
   d) Knowledge and wisdom

9. The overall Reformation view of the atonement is _____.

   a) Governmental
   b) Penal substitution
   c) Recapitulation
   d) Christus Victor

10. Which of the following held the governmental view of the atonement?

   a) James Arminius
   b) Hugo Grotius
   c) John Miley
   d) All of the above

CHAPTER 7

The Cross of Our All-Sufficient Savior: Penal Substitution

You Should Know

- Jesus's statement that the Passover cup is now his blood indicates that his death is a priestly, substitutionary death on our behalf.

- In Isaiah 53 Christ is portrayed as the Suffering Servant who wins our victory by identifying *with* us to die *for* us by becoming our penal substitute.

- The cross is absolutely necessary to redeem us, apart from it there is no holy and just forgiveness of our sins.

- Scripture: God's interpretation of his mighty acts through human authors which authoritatively gives us the meaning and significance of the events in question

- Four lines of evidence that indicate that Jesus knew he was the Messiah: His use of the title "Son of Man"; the application of Isaiah 61 to himself; his prediction that the bridegroom would be "taken away"; and the comparison of himself with Jonah and to the serpent in the wilderness

- Five Scriptural references and events that teach that the Father deliberately sacrificed his Son for us: Isaiah 53:10, John 3:16, Romans 8:32, Jesus's prayer in Gethsemane, and Jesus's cry from the cross

Essay Questions

Short

1. What evidence does the author provide that the cross is at the center of the New Testament? Why is this remarkable in light of Jewish and Roman views on crucifixion?

2. What does the Last Supper communicate about the nature of Jesus's death and his understanding of his death? What role does Gethsemane play in understanding Jesus's death for us? What do we learn from Jesus's words at Gethsemane?

3. What insight(s) does Jesus's cry from the cross ("My God, my God, why have you forsaken me?") give us about his saving work?

Long

1. Why is penal substitution the interpretation of atonement that best explains the "facts" of the cross? How does penal substitution best explain Jesus's own understanding of the cross? Choose examples from three of the "facts" described by Wellum.

Quiz

1. (T/F) Theologizing about God's mighty acts must occur within the Bible's storyline, content, and framework.

2. (T/F) For the Romans, crucifixion was reserved for aristocrats, public officials, and the wealthier members of society.

3. (T/F) In the Gospels, the apostles could not conceive of Jesus as a Suffering Servant who must die.

4. (T/F) Jesus's trial followed all of the rules and regulations for a Jewish court proceeding.

5. (T/F) If God is not the perfect standard of goodness and justice, the ground for objective morality is undercut.

6. From the perspective of Jesus and the New Testament authors,
_____ is probably the most important text in the prophetic literature for interpreting the cross.

   a) Isaiah 53
   b) Genesis 3
   c) Psalm 2
   d) 1 Kings 9:4–5

7. In the Old Testament, the _____ is linked with the pouring out of God's wrath, his judicial sentence against human sin.

   a) Snake
   b) Cup
   c) Harp
   d) Tabernacle

8. Jesus died for us as our _____ and substitute.

   a) Covenant representative
   b) Lawgiver
   c) Encourager
   d) Moral example

9. Penal substitution views the true object of the cross as _____.

   a) Sin
   b) Victory over the devil
   c) Moral progress
   d) God Himself

10. Scripture teaches that God's law mirrors _____ and is therefore inextricably related to his personal, moral, and holy character.

   a) God's revelation
   b) God's presence
   c) God's salvation
   d) God's nature

ANSWER KEY

1. T, 2. F, 3. T, 4. F, 5. T, 6. A, 7. B, 8. A, 9. D, 10. D

CHAPTER 8

The Cross of Our Glorious Redeemer: Penal Substitution, Part 2

You Should Know

- Under the old covenant, God entered into relationship with his people, and through the Levitical priesthood and sacrificial system, God granted forgiveness to them as they believed God's promises.

- God has brought us out of a state of enmity into a state of renewed fellowship with him by the cross.

- Two reasons given in the book of Hebrews that Christ is greater than the old covenant priests: Christ transcends the entire Levitical order and Christ fulfills all that the Levitical priests typified

- The legal basis of the new covenant: the blood of God's own Son

- The clearest statement that the Old Testament blood sacrifices had a substitutionary intent: Leviticus 17:11

- Three relationships that are reconciled as a result of the cross: humans' relationship with God; humans' relationship with each other; humans' relationship with creation

Essay Questions

Short

1. What does Romans 3:21–26 teach about the necessity of the

cross? What does Hebrews 9:15–28 contribute to our understanding of the necessity of the cross?

2. What does the term *propitiation* tell us about Christ's work on the cross? How does Wellum respond to the objections raised against the traditional understanding of the term by Green and Baker?

3. What evidence does Wellum provide that the term *redemption* involves payment of a price and not merely deliverance or liberation?

Long

1. Explain at least three ways that Christ's cross meets our deepest needs as human beings.

Quiz

1. (T/F) Given who the triune covenant Lord is and the nature of human sin, the only way God can redeem us is by Christ alone.

2. (T/F) God never intended the old covenant to ultimately redeem us.

3. (T/F) Due to our human limitations, all talk about God is analogical rather than univocal.

4. (T/F) At the heart of the term "justification" is the picture of a law court.

5. Christ is greater than Old Testament priests because he fulfills all that the _____ typified. (226)

    a) Levitical priests
    b) Minor prophets
    c) Major prophets
    d) Psalmists

6. The true biblical test of any theology is whether it accounts for all of the _____.

    a) Options
    b) Ways it could be misinterpreted

c) Biblical data

d) Past opinions of Christian thinkers

7. The book of Hebrews sets Jesus's sacrificial death in the larger context of _____. (p. 231)

a) The biblical covenants

b) Priesthood

c) Sin and guilt

d) All of the above

8. The Passover is more than a demonstration of God's love — it also involves the idea of _____.

a) Regeneration

b) Perseverance

c) Substitution

d) Solidarity

9. The Bible's storyline declares that humans are, due to their sin, in a state of _____ to God.

a) Indifference

b) Responsibility

c) Love

d) Hostility

10. Theological liberalism often reduces the work of the cross to _____, ignoring all of the other biblical imagery.

a) Victory

b) A moral example

c) A governmental view

d) Penal substitution

CHAPTER 9

Chalcedonian Unity: Agreement on Christ's Exclusive Identity in the Reformation

You Should Know

- "Who do people say the Son of Man is?" (Matt 16:13)

- The classic Chalcedonian formulation of the relation between the deity and humanity of Christ is "Two natures, one person."

- Modalism taught Christ is not a distinct person from the Father and Spirit.

- Three things the Chalcedonian Definition sought to do: curb speculation, clarify the use of language between East and West, and function as a definitive road map for all later christological reflection

- Docetism: Christ only appeared to be a man

- Adoptionism: Jesus was not the eternal Son made flesh but a mere man empowered by the Logos

Essay Questions

Short

1. Choose three of the seven heresies listed in this section and summarize them. How did the Chalcedonian Definition address them?

2. Summarize the first three points that capture the heart of the Chalcedonian Definition, and briefly explain why each is significant.

3. Summarize points four and five of the heart of the Chalcedonian Definition, and briefly explain why each is significant.

Long

1. What are some of the things you learned about Christ's nature in this section that you didn't know before? Choose two or three and explain what they are, and why you believe they are significant.

Quiz

1. (T/F) Confusion about who Christ is and what he has done is a matter of life and death.

2. (T/F) The Roman Church and the Reformers disagreed on issues of Trinitarian and christological orthodoxy.

3. (T/F) Chalcedon asserted that the Father and Son possessed two separate natures.

4. (T/F) Even while incarnate, the Son continued to possess all the divine attributes and perform all of his divine functions.

5. (T/F) Jesus of Nazareth would have existed even if the Son had not entered Mary's womb.

6. (T/F) After Chalcedon, further clarifications of some points brought greater christological precision.

7. Among the mistaken understandings of Jesus in his day was/were that:

    a) He was John the Baptist come back from the dead
    b) He was one of the Old Testament prophets
    c) Both A & B
    d) Neither A nor B

8. Christian christological orthodoxy is represented by the _____.

   a) Chalcedonian Definition
   b) Nicene Definition
   c) Augustinian Definition
   d) Athanasian Definition

9. Within God the Son incarnate there is no blend of natures that produces some kind of _____.

   a) Trinity
   b) Third Thing
   c) Heresy
   d) Divine Person

10. In God the Son incarnate, the divine and human attributes coexist in _____.

   a) Three persons
   b) Two persons
   c) Six dimensions
   d) One person

CHAPTER 10

The Sufficiency of Christ: The Reformation's Disagreement with Rome

You Should Know

- The Reformers' main disagreement with Rome was Rome's sacramental theology.

- Grace is the beginning, the middle, and the end of the entire work of salvation; it is totally devoid of human merit.

- The Reformers rejected Rome's sacramental theology, because they insisted that it undermined the sufficiency of Christ's work.

- Four Roman Catholic beliefs that the Reformers rejected: its sacramental theology of infused grace; *ex opere operato* administration of the sacraments; the role of the church in bestowing faith on its people; and all of the accoutrements that are tied to the entire system

- Transubstantiation: By the consecration of the elements of the Lord's Supper their substance is changed into the substance of Christ's body and blood.

- Socinianism: a sixteenth and seventeenth century movement that rejected Christ's unique identity and the sufficiency of his work

Essay Questions

Short

1. How did the Reformers understand the unity of the person and

work of Christ in relation to our salvation? How did their view contrast with the Roman Catholic view?

2. What criticisms did the Reformers make of the Roman Catholic Mass? Which Scriptures did they cite to contest it?

3. In addition to their battle against Roman Catholic theology, what other theological challenges did the Reformers face? What ultimately resulted from these challenges?

Long

1. What does "nature-grace" signify in Roman Catholic theology? How does this contrast with the Reformers' approach to grace? How does Roman Catholic theology differ from the theology of the Reformers in relation to how Christ's work is applied to us in salvation?

Quiz

1. (T/F) Rome confessed the exclusivity of Christ, but it lacked an equal emphasis on the sufficiency of his work.

2. (T/F) The Reformers embraced the nature-grace scheme of Rome.

3. (T/F) In the Roman Catholic view, as a "second Christ," the church mediates God's grace to people in and through the sacraments.

4. (T/F) By the Spirit, Christ directly applies his work to us through his priestly intercession.

5. (T/F) Calvin argued that the Mass was an affirmation of the exclusive priesthood of Christ.

6. In medieval theology, _____ were viewed as _____ for our salvation because it is through them that Christ's work becomes ours and we are infused with Christ's righteousness.

    a) Prayers / Recommended
    b) The Sacraments / Necessary
    c) Pilgrimages / Prescribed
    d) Confessions / Compulsory

7. In Rome's theology, there is never _____, but only *Christus in ecclesia* (Christ in the church) and *ecclesia in Christo* (the church in Christ).

    a) *Solus Christus* (Christ alone)
    b) *Totus Christus* (the whole Christ)
    c) *Ex opera operato* (by the work worked)
    d) *E pluribus unum* (out of many, one)

8. _____ wrote: "I teach that people should put their trust in nothing but Jesus Christ alone, not in their prayers, merits, or their own good deeds."

    a) Johann von Staupitz
    b) Thomas Aquinas
    c) Martin Luther
    d) Pope Leo X

9. _____ in life and in death is the sole grounds of our justification.

    a) Christ's obedience
    b) Our effort
    c) The church's blessing
    d) Church attendance

10. _____ wrote: "We are justified only by believing, and receiving the righteousness of another, and not by our own works, or merit."

    a) Michael Servetus
    b) Charitie Bancroft
    c) Aquinas
    d) Ursinus

CHAPTER 11

The Loss of Christ's Exclusivity: Our Current Challenge

You Should Know

- The philosophy of our time is different from the theological philosophy of the sixteenth century, because of a radical shift in epistemology and worldview.

- With the benefit of hindsight, the Enlightenment can be said to have marked a decisive and irreversible change in the political, social, and religious outlook of Western Europe and North America.

- Two Enlightenment ideas that challenged the beliefs of the Christian church: only human reason is necessary for human knowledge, and we can make sense of the world without God's personal involvement

- The four Quests of the historical Jesus: the Old Quest, the No Quest, the New Quest, the Third Quest

- *Noumena*: in Kant's thought, objects that lie beyond our experience

- *Phenomena*: in Kant's thought, objects that are present to our experience

Essay Questions

Short

1. How did the Enlightenment view of reason influence the

Enlightenment approach to Christology? How does this contrast with the Reformers' approach to Christology?

2. Choose two of the "pillars" of Christian orthodoxy and contrast them with their corresponding principles of the historical-critical method. What difference does each make in understanding Jesus's identity?

3. Briefly summarize the four Quests of the historical Jesus. What do these Quests have in common in their approach to Scripture?

Long

1. In light of the influence of the Enlightenment on our society, which aspects of Jesus's identity are non-Christians likely to find plausible and implausible? Choose at least one point from each category.

Quiz

1. (T/F) Our theology must help the church meet the challenges we face in presenting Christ to a skeptical age.

2. (T/F) For true knowledge of God, the self, and the world, we depend upon revelation from the Creator-Covenant Lord.

3. (T/F) Kantianism accepts *a priori* the possibility that Christ is God the Son incarnate.

4. (T/F) The church's confession of Christ's exclusivity does not depend on his historicity.

5. (T/F) The historical-critical method is incapable of identifying the historical Jesus in Scripture.

6. (T/F) The trend today in historical Jesus studies is to assume that Jesus is essentially who the church says he is.

7. Sinful _____ resists the unmerited grace of a divine-human Savior.

    a) Religious hypocrisy
    b) False obedience

c) Human pride

d) Theological heresy

8. _____ viewed the enlightened person as one who reasons autonomously, without dependence upon authorities of the past.

a) Aquinas

b) Luther

c) Calvin

d) Kant

9. Kant limited knowledge to objects as they appear to us, which exclude _____.

a) Knowledge of the world

b) Knowledge about ourselves

c) Knowledge of God

d) Knowledge of time and space

10. Extratextual readings of the Gospels separate the "Jesus of history" from the _____.

a) "Jesus of the Church"

b) "Christ of faith"

c) "Messiah of the Jews"

d) "Miracle-Worker of Galilee"

CHAPTER 12

Reaffirming Christ Alone Today

You Should Know

- Postmodernism asserts that the biblical text has no stable or decidable meaning.

- A truly biblical Christology must proceed from the Bible's self-presentation of Christ.

- Postmodernism: a view that rejects "grand narratives" and universal, objective truth by which we can validate some things and invalidate others

- Two postmodern ideas that have become dominant and have impacted the church's confession of *Christ alone*: "knowledge" is merely a subjective opinion based on a local perspective; "God" is merely the non-personal and developmental dynamics of a changing world

- "Christology from below": the attempt to do Christology from the vantage point of historical-critical research and the current thought of the day

- "Christology from above": A Christology that starts with Scripture, its revelational epistemology, and the truth of the biblical worldview

Essay Questions

Short

1. According to a revelational epistemology, what is the basis of our knowledge? How does our knowledge relate to God's knowledge?

2. Briefly summarize the Enlightenment approach to knowledge. How did this view influence approaches to Scripture? How does a postmodern approach to Scripture differ from a modern approach?

3. What problems does postmodernism pose for constructing a biblical Christology? Does it end in a different place in this regard than the modernist approach to Christology?

Long

1. In light of what you've learned in this section, what are some ways that we can reach postmodern people with the message of Jesus?

Quiz

1. (T/F) In today's society, Jesus is typically viewed as the Son of God incarnate.

2. (T/F) The basis for Christ's exclusivity and sufficiency must be articulated and defended today.

3. (T/F) It is possible to have finite but objective and true knowledge.

4. (T/F) Today we cannot proclaim the work of Christ before first confronting the loss of his exclusivity that makes his sufficiency possible.

5. (T/F) We must confess today that Scripture and tradition have equal authority.

6. Most scholars acknowledge that Western culture has shifted from a modern to a _____ mindset.

   a) Premodern
   b) Postmodern
   c) Semi-Modern
   d) Futuristic

7. Postmodernism begins with the same _____ as Enlightenment modernism.

   a) Turn to the subject
   b) Turn to the object

    c) Turn from the truth

    d) Style

8. Knowledge in postmodernity is not objective and universal but _____.

    a) Mysterious and slippery

    b) Scientific and clinical

    c) Subjective and local

    d) Intuitive and emotional

9. Every interpretation of Christ's identity depends upon a presuppositional nexus of _____ commitments.

    a) Philosophical and theological

    b) Church and ministry

    c) Moral and rational

    d) Vocational and biblical

10. The church today must defend _____ and an authoritative Scripture as basically credible and absolutely necessary. (308)

    a) Trinitarian theism

    b) Sunday worship

    c) Daily Bible reading

    d) Miracles

Notes